Consolatio

Habib Tengour

Consolatio

Translated from French by
Will Harris and Delaina Haslam

poetry
translation
centre

First published in 2022
by the Poetry Translation Centre Ltd
The Albany, Douglas Way, London, SE8 4AG

www.poetrytranslation.org

Poems © Habib Tengour
English Translations © Will Harris and Delaina Haslam 2022
Introduction © Will Harris and Delaina Haslam 2022
Afterword © Shash Trevett 2022
Will Harris photo © Matthew Thompson
Habib Tengour photo © Pierre Joris

ISBN: 978-1-7398948-1-8

A catalogue record for this book is available from the British Library

Typeset in Minion by Poetry Translation Centre Ltd

Series Editor: Nashwa Gowanlock
Cover Design: Kit Humphrey
Printed in the UK by T.J. International

This publication has been supported by the European Union's Creative Europe culture programme which funds literary translations.

The Poetry Translation Centre is supported using public funding by Arts Council England.

Contents

Introduction	7
'Table'	12
Something else	16
Hesitation	18
Exodus	20
Speech	22
Cutting	24
In Heaney's Line of Sight	26
Treasure	30
The painter's studio (variations)	34
Recollection	40
Guestbook	42
Le rempart de Sebti	44
Lament	50
Ordinances	52
Banishment	54
Refrain	56
The fire	58
Afterword	61
About the contributors	64
About the series	66

Introduction

Habib Tengour was born in 1947 and uprooted from his family home in Mostaganem, Algeria, at the age of 12, when his parents' involvement in the struggle for independence led them to flee to France. They arrived in Paris two years before the 17 October massacre of 1961, when French police turned violently against a protest by pro-independence Algerians, with demonstrators being pushed into the Seine and dozens of people killed. In 'Banishment', '[t]he docks are crowded with ghosts of October'.

Other events from the colonial history of Algeria haunt Tengour's work. In 'Lament', a speaker crossing a station platform is interrupted by 'a groan in the Dahra caves'. This refers to an earlier French atrocity: on 18 June 1845, the Ouled Riah tribe were taking shelter in the caves of Dahra, when French troops barred their exit and started throwing burning sticks; once the smoke had cleared, 600 bodies – nearly all dead – were pulled out. 'Trick of the repressed, image superimposed,' runs the next line of the poem. Surface images – 'superimposed' like colonial rule – slide away; the repressed ghosts of Algerian history return.

Since his initial departure as a child, Tengour has spent the majority of his life between France and Algeria. He returned to his birthplace in 1972 to carry out his military service and then to teach at the University of Constantine, where he has been a professor of sociology and anthropology. He now spends roughly half of the year in each country.

Tengour's concept of exile is decidedly un nostalgic. *Gens de Mosta* (1997), a collection of sketches of everyday life (most of it still untranslated), takes place in Mostaganem. One of its vignettes, 'Chansons', speaks with fond irony about songs sung about the pain of emigration:

> The songs of the past were full of regret (Hasni had piles of old recordings […] which he'd unearth at the Montreuil flea market every Sunday). They lamented – systematically – those who'd emigrated to France. They constantly discouraged any attempt to leave the home country. This was simply an open door to worry, trouble, problems, and disappointments for those who undertook it. It had a name with fearsome connotations: exile. Every departure meant a decease, since, the song said, no one could live for long far from the eyes that cherished them.

'The first aspect of exile is physical, real exile,' Tengour told us in a video call during the process of translating *Consolatio*. He explained that this 'real' exile has twin manifestations. First on the personal level and, second, encompassing the collective memory of Algeria since its 19th-century conquest, when tribes were sent to penal colonies in Cayenne and New Caledonia. A later wave of exile occurred during the First World War when many Algerians emigrated to France to find work. Exile is often embodied in Tengour's poetry by the figure of Ulysses, who has wandered in and out of his writing ever since his first book *The Arc and the Star* (1978). But it also extends to the dispossession of Palestinians, and the continuing plight of other exiled peoples.

Tengour's first language is a dialectal variation of Arabic but he writes in French, the language of the coloniser. He is typically long-sighted and equivocal about this. While Malek Haddad 'condemned himself to silence' rather than write in French after independence, Tengour refuses the '"false debate" around language' – which is to say, the false equation of linguistic and national identities. In one essay, '"Postcolonial"

Narrative and Identity' (2012), he argues against identity as 'a quest for origins – Berber, Arabo-Islamic, Mediterranean or other – or as the recovery of some lost (forever!) property – the authenticity of lineage'. Like the poet Mohammed Dib, he takes 'French as the writing language in which to reconstruct identity in exile'. And perhaps French makes sense for Tengour precisely because it is so compromised. If we feel 'authenticity' in his work, it derives not from a sense of 'lineage' but from the quality of expression.

In any case, the consequences of writing in French – and the role of speech more generally – reverberate through *Consolatio*. 'Treasure' draws from Kateb Yacine's novel *Le Polygone étoilé* (1966), describing the impossible desire to appease a French-speaking teacher and an Arabic-speaking mother. Yacine would later turn to popular theatre and dialectal Arabic. But incompleteness does not appear as an undesirable characteristic in Tengour's work; in fact, incompleteness could be said to form a site of desire, the founding principle of his exilic identity. He holds both the teacher and mother within himself. This is because – beyond the fact of the mother also, of course, being a kind of teacher – power cannot be escaped by some filial retreat. Completeness is illusory.

In 1981, Tengour published his playful, influential manifesto 'Le Surréalisme maghrébin' (translated as 'Maghribi Surrealism' by Pierre Joris), which sought to shift the locus of surrealism away from André Breton and Paris and to align it with the subversive history of Sufism and its 'pure psychic automatism, mad love, revolt, unanticipated encounters, etc'. It made sense to him that a people defined by exile ('homeland a confiscated identity') would embrace a poetry of dreams, arbitrary rules, and humour. 'Indeed there does exist a divided space called the Maghrib,' writes Tengour, 'but the Maghribian is always elsewhere. And that is where he fulfils himself.' As he says in the opening poem: 'Acrostics are good. An automatic trigger. Words must come and put themselves where they should be.' There is a tradition of letting words 'put themselves where they should be' going back at least to the acrostics of the medieval poet Yosef Ibn Abitur. Form is, in Tengour's words, what 'permits content to reach its goal, namely to procure the jubilation listening gives us'. And that jubilation – emerging from 'the tragic experience of the colonised', always elsewhere – is what his poems leave us with.

Tengour's work has been translated previously by Pierre Joris (with whom he also edited *Poems for the Millennium: University of California Book of North African Literature* in 2012) and by Marilyn Hacker. This introduction makes use of Joris's translations of Tengour's essays included in *Exile Is My Trade: A Habib Tengour Reader* (Black Widow Press, 2012). When embarking on our collaborative translation of Tengour's poetry, we were keen to turn to newer, untranslated work. We chose *Consolatio* (yet to be published in French) for its mix of playful poem-puzzles and longer prose poems reflecting on forms of loss. A 'consolatio' is a form of classical rhetoric used to console mourners. Tengour's book contains numerous tributes – some of which he has read at funerals – to deceased writers and friends including Tahar Djaout, Youcef Sebti, Abedlkader Alloula, Bakhti Benouada, and the painter Abdallah Benanteur and his poet-painter wife Monique Boucher.

Our approach to the collaboration involved both of us working from the French. We would each take the same poem to translate over a period of a week or two, then hold a video conference to compare and merge our versions. Thank you to Habib for his patience and generosity in responding to our questions over the course of putting this book together. And thank you to the series editors at the Poetry Translation Centre for their thoughtful feedback and support throughout.

                         Will Harris and Delaina Haslam

Poems

> « O Table, ma console et ma consolatrice, pourquoi, table, aujourd'hui me deviens-tu urgente ? »
> Francis Ponge

La table, pas vraiment, ou alors celle de n'importe quel bistro. Une Kneipe, pas tout à fait ça !
Parce que le bureau est un foutoir. Pas l'atelier idéal où se construit patiemment le poème. Vision romantique démentie par le temps.
Pas de console, pas de consolation. Pas dramatique non plus.
Mohammed Dib me disait se mettre à sa table de travail tous les jours. Faire ses gammes sans état d'âme. Un boulot de fonctionnaire. Il est vrai que Dib avait le souci de construire une œuvre sourd aux impondérables du quotidien. Il s'en donnait la peine…
Beaucoup d'amis sont partis laissant le pain sur la planche… Et l'exil comme un rouleau concasseur…
…
Ton contexte diffère. Bien que… ici, à Uhlandstraße tu disposes d'un bureau de ministre où consolider ton imaginaire. Tu n'as jamais disposé d'un tel confort. Mais tu préfères bricoler…
Tu poses le portable sur les genoux ou la table de cuisine évitant les miettes de pain taper textes manuscrits sur prospectus. Tu laisses traîner le texte des mois pour le reprendre aujourd'hui jour anniversaire.
Ecris comme cela vient.

> 'O Table, my console and my consoler, why, table, do you become urgent to me today?'
> Francis Ponge

Table. Not really. Or if so one you'd find in any old cafe. Though not quite a Kneipe.
Because my office is a dump. It's not the perfect studio in which to patiently craft a poem. A romantic vision belied by time.
No console, no consolation. No drama either.
Mohammed Dib told me he'd go to his desk every day. Practising his scales without fuss. A civil servant's job. Dib wished to write his works oblivious to the hitches and snags of everyday life. He made the effort.
Many friends have gone leaving their work unfinished. And exile is like a hammer mill.
…
Your context is different. Here in Uhlandstraße, you have a minister's office to consolidate your imagination. You've never known such comfort. But you prefer to make do.
You put your laptop on your knee or the kitchen table avoiding crumbs, typing up text scrawled on flyers. You leave a piece for months to pick it up again today on your birthday.
You write as it comes.

Tu les forces à venir. Les mots. N'importe où. N'importe quel support.
Pas de rituel particulier. Inefficace depuis longtemps.
C'est mieux quand tu feuillettes un livre qu'un terme accroche ton regard oreille. Tu grappilles.
Monde muet et monde volubile t'intiment de dire. Dictent leurs lois. Leurs voix ? Qu'est-ce à dire ? Tu traînes !
Ça urge.
Sans les dictionnaires, comment faire ?
A croire ton cerveau vide de son lexique. A vrai dire, tu n'as jamais brillé par l'éloquence, la richesse du vocabulaire. Certains mots, certaines tournures te surprennent. Tu dois chercher longtemps. Ce n'est pas ta langue… (de quelle langue tu parles ?) Parles-tu encore ?
Devant ton bout de papier, tu ne sais pas vraiment ce que tu as écrire. Tu retardes le moment. Il te manquait le thrène de Nabile maintenant encore Nono… Les vis-à-vis s'éteignent.
L'acrostiche est un bon truc. Déclenchement automatique. Les lettres initiales posées surtout ne pas réfléchir. Les mots sont obligés de venir se placer là où ils doivent être… Une transe.

Tout cela ne peut avoir lieu sans le choc préalable qui te cloue dans l'instant sans voix.
Apprentissage d'un chant / un hymne pour mémoire

Athènes, mercredi 11 mai 2016 – Le Kremlin-Bicêtre, vendredi 10 mars 2017 – Luxembourg, vendredi 31 mars 2017 – Berlin, mercredi 13 septembre 2017 – dimanche 9 octobre 2017 – mercredi 22 novembre 2017 – Le Kremlin-Bicêtre, jeudi 21 décembre 2017 – Berlin, Uhlandstraße, jeudi 29 mars 2018.

You force them out. Words. Anywhere. Writing on whatever. No particular ritual. Ineffective for a long time now.
It works best when you flick through a book and a word catches your eye, your ear. You glean.
The *silent world* and the voluble world order you to speak. They dictate their laws. Their voices? What does this mean? You drag your feet.
It's urgent.
With no dictionaries, what can you do?
You'd think your brain was empty of vocabulary. To be honest, you never stood out for your eloquence or rich lexicon. Certain words, certain turns of phrase come to you. You have to search a long time. This isn't your language ... (of which language do you speak?) Do you speak still?
Before your piece of paper, you don't really know what you're going to write. You put off the moment. You missed out on Nabile's threnody, and now Nono's … Face-to-face meetings are dying out.
Acrostics are good. An automatic trigger. Initial letters placed more than anything not to think about it. Words must come and put themselves where they should be. A trance.

None of this can happen without the prior shock that nails you to the instant without a voice.
Learning a song / a hymn to memory

Athens, Wednesday 11 May 2016 – Le Kremlin-Bicêtre, Friday 10 March 2017 – Luxembourg, Friday 31 March 2017 – Berlin, Wednesday 13 September 2017 – Sunday 9 October 2017 – Wednesday 22 November 2017 – Le Kremlin-Bicêtre, Thursday 21 December 2017 – Berlin, Uhlandstraße, Thursday 29 March 2018.

Autre chose

Soudain le jour
Moindre jour
Rappel à ne pas baisser la garde
Familiarité des choses n'est pas habitude
Ni fruit d'imagination

Dib partage avec Guillevic le goût d'*autre chose*
Chose entre autres objets à l'étal
Sans prix indiqué ni nommée
Accoutrement singulier d'un carnaval révolu
Clef du festin à l'abandon

Poésie poursuit son cours s'interrompt
Intervalle irrégulomadaire ce qui laisse
Perplexe devant le masque suspendu
À l'entrée de la gare désaffectée
Après la catastrophe

Messager d'un Olympe abîmé
Quels mots propices
Invoquer la pureté d'Hélène transportée en Egypte
À l'insu des Grecs et de Troie enivrés par
La douceur du duvet de l'aimée.

Rappelle-toi la promenade sur le rivage
Iliade et Odyssée ininterrompues
Le temps que dure l'accolade

Autrefois insiste sur la candeur de l'écume

Something else

Suddenly the day
The least day
Reminds you not to lower your guard
Familiarity of things is not habit
Or figment of the imagination

Dib shares with Guillevic a taste for *autre chose*
Among other things on the stall
No price marked or named
Singular outfit of a carnival past
Key to the abandoned feast

Poetry follows its course is interrupted
Every-so-often intervals leaving
You puzzled in front of the mask hanging
At the entrance to the disused station
After the disaster

Herald of a ruined Olympus
Such auspicious words
To invoke the purity of Helen taken to Egypt
Unbeknownst to the Greeks and Troy intoxicated by
The soft fuzz of love's down.

Remember the walk on the shore
Iliad and Odyssey uninterrupted
For the duration of the embrace

Time accentuates the white froth

Hésitation

La parole
Parle avec le temps
Son temps de parole

Émergence d'un visage   Une étendue
Ce qui manque ?

Parole parlant au corps
Exprimant sa présence dans une langue remmaillée
Le trait traverse la voûte

Le coloris
Par la suite rehausse le regard

Invite à converser   / Contemplation

Mis en garde   les mots ne viennent pas
Des intonations   Des silences

Tu n'es pas là pour forcer une frontière.

Hesitation

Speech
Speaks over time
It has a speaking time

Emergence of a face   A scope
What is missing?

Speech speaking to the body
Expressing presence in a repaired tongue
The line spans the vault

The colouring
Thereafter enhances the look

Invites talk   / Contemplation

Warned   the words do not come
Intonation   Silence

You're not here to force open a border

Exode

Nostalgie   de   Du Bellay   Ritsos   Darwich
Constance du timbre
Exil bat la mesure
Retrouve une voie dans le chant

Les parents seraient-ils exilés
Pas les enfants ?
Transmission d'un inouï
Mutisme du père   / plaintes maternelles

Emigrer par manque de pain est-ce s'exiler ?
Question idiote
L'exil s'ancre dans la colonie   / Discours

Dramatiser la rupture
L'eau versée sur le perron console du départ

Promesse d'un retour

Exodus

Nostalgia   for   Du Bellay   Ritsos   Darwish
Constant tone
Exile keeps time
Finds a route back in song

Would the parents be exiled
Not the children?
Transmission of the unheard
Silence of the father   / maternal complaints

Is emigrating for lack of bread exile?
Stupid question
Exile is anchored in the colony   / Discourse

Dramatise the rupture
Water poured on the front steps consoles the departure

Promise of return

Parole

La parole parle le temps d'émerger
Souci flagrant histoire sans paroles
Défaillance dans le sursaut

La main parle au corps un flot
Dans ce corps elle persiste s'ancre
D'un jet traverse l'apparence

Les couleurs ajoutées à la hâte
Agrémentent la caresse
Invitent à goûter

Les mots se retranchent derrière la barricade
Etat d'urgence   / parole suspendue
Naturellement

Tu n'es pas là pour heurter la porte

Speech

Speech speaks the time to emerge
Bad anxiety history without words
Failure from the start

The hand speaks to the body a flow
In the body, it persists anchors
In one leap spanning the appearance

Colours added in haste
Embellish the caress
Invite to taste

Words retreat behind the barricade
State of emergency   / speech suspended
Of course

You're not here to beat against the door

Découpe

Beaucoup
l'œil darde ses rayons
glissent doucement ces floraisons souhaitées
dans la migration

Difficile
à nommer ce qui sépare
au moment de se quitter
n'est pas encore

Au-dessus
blessure d'une lame trempée
dans la coupe l'été
le sel des sirènes

Plus tard
matière dérobée à la nuit
tu saisis une paire de ciseaux
découpes ce qui reste en rondelles

Cutting

Many
rays of the eye dart
those desired blooms gliding smoothly
in migration

Difficult
to name what becomes separate
at the moment of parting
not yet

Above
injury from a hardened blade
in the cut the summer
the sirens' salt

Later
matter stolen from the night
you grab a pair of scissors
cut what remains to pieces

Dans la Ligne de Mire de Monsieur Heaney

1. Prise de contact

Se donner une contrainte à l'
Ecoute du poème   ta voix d'
Au-delà   humble offrande au
Monde   ceux que les mots troublent
Unis dans la jouissance d'un partage
Secret   cela sans doute

Hélas je ne connaissais pas tes mots
Epris pourtant de ton nom
Ainsi des rencontres
Nouées dans l'ignorance
Entre *les brancards et le sillon* les
Yeux écarquillés sur la grand-route

2. Vivre dans la distance

Les ombres de nos amis s'agitent dans les rues
Nous rappeler ce moment précis
Basculement du désir dans une poussière
De toute part percée de soleil

Nous les retrouvons au bar cadenassé
De la pêcherie   heures joyeuses
Où le juge côtoie l'indic
Chacun son cageot sur la toile cirée

In Heaney's Line of Sight

1. First contact

Setting myself a constraint when the poem hits my
Ear   your voice
A voice beyond   humble offering to the
Many   those who words disturb
United in the joy of a shared
Secret   yes no doubt

How sad not to know your words
Enamoured though I was with your name
And so encounters were
Nestled in ignorance *betw-*
Een the shafts and the furrow the
Yards-long stare down the main road

2. Living in the distance

Our friends' shadows mill in the streets
To remind us of this specific moment
Shifting desire in a speck of dust
Pierced by the sun on all sides

We find them at the padlocked bar
Of the fishing ground   happy hours
Where the judge meets the snitch
Each has a crate on the oilcloth

C'est un salmigondis   aigre-doux
Héritage d'une décennie absence d'amuse-gueules

Les serviettes en papier aux couleurs vives font un
Arc en ciel   / bienvenue   au seuil semé d'étoiles

Une soirée décevante malgré les préparatifs de noce

3. Le temps de se mettre en route

Je ne connais pas le lieu
A l'embouchure de quels fleuves ?

J'ai appris dans ton pays
Les morts passent dans la neige
Pour rassurer le rêveur chagriné

Ils parlent une langue de feu et de pierre
S'abreuvent avec l'oiseau dans des tasses ébréchées

Je sais qu'ils s'acheminent vers l'Ouest
Quand c'est l'heure du départ
Que les cendres refroidissent dans la cheminée

L'exil pointe sa mitrailleuse
Un vide t'épuise à la douane
La fiche à remplir te laisse perplexe

Au matin une eau calme reflète un amour
Invitation à traverser

It's a mishmash   bitter-sweet
Legacy of a decade without appetisers

The brightly coloured napkins make a
Rainbow   / welcome   to the star-strewn threshold

The evening disappoints in spite of preparations for the wedding

3. As we set off

I don't know the place
At the mouth of which rivers?

I learned in your country
The dead pass in the snow
To reassure the troubled dreamer

They speak a language of fire and stone
They drink with the birds from chipped cups

I know they are heading west
When it is time to leave
The ashes cool in the fireplace

Exile aims its machine gun
Emptiness exhausts you at customs
The form to fill out confuses you

In the morning a calm water reflects a love
Invitation to cross

Trésor

Sémillante.
…
Ainsi Yacine décrit son institutrice.   Etincellement et semailles,
L'impression est immédiate.   Etoilement.
                              Feu follet au tableau noir

L'enfant s'accroche à la grande ourse.
        De la luge sur la voie lactée, chimère.
            Bonjour, bonjour, bonjour, bonjour, bonjour

Tout un monde se découvre après le 8 mai 45 / dans la prison
Un peuple   une patrie   / et la vie
                        Etoile blottie dans ton paletot

L'édifice ordonne l'espace fragmentaire du songe

Cela invite au recueillement.
            Non pas prière, mais   concentration
            Dévotion absente
            Seule importe l'attention

Merveilleusement,
Comme la huppe de la reine de Saba dans son envol elle
Bouscule les divinités des tribus elle
Défait des armées aguerries
Son cri encourage les blessés à résister.
Inviolables,
Les trois pierres disposées en âtre et la quatrième

Treasure

Sémillante.

…

That's how Yacine describes his teacher. Brilliance and shimmer,
The impression is immediate.   Incandescence.
                              Blackboard sprite

The child clings to the great bear.
        Sledding on the milky way, chimera.
                Bonjour, bonjour, bonjour, bonjour, bonjour

A whole world was discovered after 8 May 1945 / in prison
A people   a homeland   / and life
                              Star nestled in your overcoat

The building orders the fragmentary space of the dream

Which summons thought.
                Not prayer, but   concentration
                Without devotion
                Attention is all that matters

Marvellously,
Like the Queen of Sheba's hoopoe in flight she
Shakes up the gods of the tribes she
Defeats seasoned armies
Her cry calls the wounded to resist
Impregnable,
The three stones arranged in the hearth and the fourth

                                    Autel du lignage
                  Autour, une vague trace

Ceux qui défilent dans l'espoir d'une révélation sont déçus
L'âpreté des lieux déconcerte.
Tu rentres éreinté

Acclamations,
Elles sèment un doute dans le vêtement de la victoire.
Une mélancolie contrainte à céder le passage.

                              Ancestral shrine
               Around it, a faint line

Those who march in hope of revelation are disappointed
The brutality of places confounds.
You come home exhausted

The cheering,
It sows doubt in the victory garment.
Melancholy forced to give way.

L'atelier du peintre
(variations)

Abdallah dit : quand je le regarde le tableau m'engueule de ne pas être à la hauteur des cimaises, de ne voir que la couleur au lieu du trait, de glisser sur la toile content de mon élan alors qu'il fallait s'accrocher, non pas à une forme, mais à la matière difficile à extraire du tube.

Que viens-tu faire dans l'atelier ?

Ici, il faut peindre non pas rêver peinture. Tu n'as personne de qui tenir.
Laisse ta tête au carrefour, elle affiche trop une identité étrangère à ce lieu.
A la rigueur la main pourra faire l'affaire mais fiche-lui la paix.

Le tableau, moi, je l'emmerde ! clame Abdallah
même s'il a raison.

***

Bien sûr, la peinture ne ment pas
elle ne dit pas non plus la vérité à proprement parler
elle ne discute pas ni ne suggère quelque intuition à étaler
    au grand jour.
Ce qu'elle veut je n'en sais rien
à moi de me débrouiller avec mes pinceaux
or je me suis toujours levé très tôt.

The painter's studio (variations)

Abdallah says: when I look at it the painting yells at me for not being on its level, for seeing only colour instead of line, for gliding across the canvas happy with the forms I achieve when I should be fixed on the substance that's so hard to squeeze from the tube.

What are you doing in the studio?

Here, you have to paint not dream about painting. You have no one to follow.
Leave your head at the junction, it looks far too foreign for this place.
If necessary, the hand can do it but leave it be.

Fuck it! shouts Abdallah, though the painting
might be right

***

Because, of course, the painting doesn't lie
it's not telling the truth either
it neither argues nor brings some intuition into the
    light.
What it wants I don't know
I just take my brushes and work it
out but I've always got up early.

***

Dois-je m'obstiner. Je ne dois rien.
Je l'ai compris sitôt posé pied à Paris.
J'ai eu beaucoup de chance mais j'ai travaillé sans me
    souiller des galeristes.
Je voulais peindre et je continue à peindre.
Je me lève toujours aussi tôt.
Cela est nécessaire
non, il faut produire.

***

Ah, *te voilà !*
C'est comme ça que la toile m'accueille quand je
    m'approche du chevalet.
Quand elle ne prononce pas des grossièretés comme *le con arrive* !
J'ai toujours pris ça pour une provocation
et j'ai relevé le défi
mais j'aurais peut-être mieux fait de quitter l'atelier
et admettre une fois pour toute
cette évidence :
immanquablement, nous n'étions pas naît pour peindre.

***

***

Do I have to persist. I owe nothing.
I knew this as soon as I set foot in Paris.
I was very lucky but I worked without dirtying my hands
    with gallery owners.
I wanted to paint and I continue to paint.
I still get up early.
That is necessary
no, you have to produce.

***

Ah, there you are!
This is how the canvas greets me when I approach the
    easel.
When it's not uttering filth like *it's that cunt again*!
I have always taken that as a provocation
and taken up the challenge
but maybe I should have left the studio
and admitted once and for all
this blatant truth:
inevitably, we weren't born to paint.

***

Lorsque je peins ou que je grave ma main fait tout le travail.
Ce qui est difficile, c'est de s'arrêter.
Ça bouleverse le rythme.
Quand on reprend, c'est autre chose.
Le bleu devient vert et les personnages disparaissent.
La main recompose le cadre dans un nouveau geste.
que faire ? Recommencer

***

Laissez le peintre chercher ce qui est bea**u**

***

Autrement tracer un rêv**e**

***

Heureusement Monique est là.
Elle travaille.
Son atelier jouxte le sien.
La toile ne lui dit rien mais attend sagement de voir
– dans le clignement où mensonge semble vrai
la couleur
s'incarner dans le dessin.

Let's consider the matter of paint or engraving my hand
    does all the work.
What is difficult is to stop.
It upsets the rhythm.
When you return, it's something else.
Blue turns green and figures disappear.
With new gestures your hand remakes the scene –
question why? Start over

***

Let the painter seek the visual aperçu

***

Any means at least to trace the dream's image

***

Here is Monique at last.
She's working.
Her studio is next to his.
The canvas tells her little but waits
patiently to see – in the blink
when untruth seems true –
colour embody the drawn lines.

Souvenance

Bourrasque à souhait /   Arrachement
Toiture résiste au déluge

Ici arbre veille
Ses feuilles persistantes

Je n'aurai pas sombré dans le caniveau
Œil indifférent aux réverbérations du soir

Stratagème s'extirper du dédale
Éviter s'incendier ailes et vaisseaux

Celui-là – sous terre – sans recours

Recollection

Gust at will /   Uprooting
Roof withstands the flood

Here tree keeps watch
Its leaves ever green

No I did not sink in the gutter
Eye indifferent to evening's reflections

Ruse to escape the labyrinth
Avoid burning wings and ships

This one – underground – without recourse

Livre d'or

Sûrement là tapie dans l'aurore amarante
Guet   offrande attachée de fils d'ors

Les Anciens convoqués à la fête
S'apprêtent à rugir au signal

Machinerie parée d'effets spéciaux

Le livre d'images aspire dans une vase
Rouille /   divagation nourrie de sucre candi

Asseoir un soupir au bord du bitume
En un clin d'œil ton corps s'ébrèche…

Guestbook

Surely hiding there in morning amaranth
Lying in wait   offering tied with gold threads

The Elders summoned to the party
Ready themselves to roar at the signal

Machinery adorned with special effects

The book of images breathes in silt
Rust-red / rock-candy-fed rambling

Sets down a sigh beside the asphalt
In the blink of an eye your body is cracked.

Le rempart de Sebti

« Mes feux du quartier pauvre
éclairent l'avenir »
Jean Sénac, Alger-Reclus, 1971-1972

La photo se trouve dans l'*Anthologie de la nouvelle poésie algérienne*, de Jean Sénac, parue en 1971 dans le n°14 de *Poésie 1*. Ho Chi Min j'ai pensé. Un côté maquisard – le treillis – frêle mais résolu. Résolument ancrée dans cette époque chargée de nos rêves flamboyants, de l'innocence de nos matins en fête...
Le poème *Nuit de noce* m'a touché révolte et pudeur sans concession au machisme algérien…
A Alger, Sénac m'a beaucoup parlé de Sebti de sa droiture de sa rigueur de sa ténacité à comprendre. …
A Barika, officier de la Révolution Agraire empêtré dans les fourchettes, me revenaient souvent ces vers j'en mesurais la justesse :

« Toi /
    tes semblables /
    vous qui sabotez la réforme agraire. »

Je partageais ta hargne de pauvre devant l'arrogance des nantis…
…
Longtemps plus tard, en juin 1979, J'ai fait la connaissance de Sebti aux Rencontres Poétiques organisées par Abdelkader

Le rempart de Sebti

> 'My beacons of the poor
> quarters light up the future'
> Jean Sénac, Alger-Reclus, 1971–1972

The photo is in Jean Sénac's *Anthology of New Algerian Poetry* of 1971, which appeared in the 14th edition of *Poésie 1*. Ho Chi Minh, I thought. A maquisard look – fatigues – frail but resolute. Resolutely anchored in that era filled with our blazing dreams, with the innocence of feast-day mornings.
The poem 'Nuit de noce' made an impression on me – modesty and revolt – without concession to Algerian machismo.
In Algiers, Sénac spoke a lot to me of Sebti – his integrity, his rigour, his determination to understand.
In Barika, as an officer of the agrarian revolution mired in the business of property exclusions, these lines came to me often. They struck me for their aptness:

> 'You /
> those like you /
> you who butcher agrarian reform.'

I shared your poor man's hostility to the arrogance of the well-off.
…
Much later, in June 1979, I met Sebti at the *Rencontres poétiques* organised by Abdelkader Djeghloul at the CDSH in Oran. Or

Djeghloul au CDSH d'Oran. Ou peut-être en 1980. Il y avait beaucoup de monde des deux côtés de la tribune.
Beaucoup d'agitation…
Chahut bon enfant tout le monde voulait lire sans préséance…
Beaucoup d'enthousiasme dans l'amphithéâtre…
Beaucoup d'insouciance aussi…
Le bar en face du centre restait ouvert tard. Personne ne soupçonnait alors ce qui allait suivre… A moins que le regard anxieux de Sebti…   Ailleurs et présent
…que cherchait-il à nous dire avec son *Homme forgeron* ?
Notre aîné élaborait un système du monde peu probant. Etait-il visionnaire ou sombrait-il encore dans *la folie* ?
Avec Djaout et Skif et Touati et Laghouati et… on s'esclaffait au comptoir, tournée après tournée, sourds à l'appel. Gênés, toutefois. Nous reconnaissions le poète insurgé. Et renouveler la tournée…
On rigolait quand même…
L'enfer, chez lui, n'est pas qu'une figure de style.
Et quand il dit :

> « Sur le sentier d'une lutte /
> j'ai débouché sur la folie /
> j'ai plongé dans la folie / … »

nous étions convaincus de la véracité du propos.
…
Le connaissant mieux, je découvre un intellectuel écorché vif, interrogeant sans cesse. Invité à une table ronde de notre laboratoire de l'URASC sur les mouvements réformistes en Islam, il présente une communication sur « la notion d'aliénation chez Malek Bennabi », je ne retrouve malheureusement plus le texte. Son savoir du salafisme m'étonne, à un moment où peu d'entre nous s'y intéressent…
« Il faut te mettre sérieusement à l'arabe, me dit-il à la pause-café. Autrement tu resteras toujours infirme » …

maybe 1980. There were many people on either side of the stage.
Much noise.
A friendly commotion. Everyone wanted to read with no order of precedence. There was much enthusiasm in the auditorium. Much insouciance too.
The bar opposite the centre stayed open late. No one guessed then what was going to happen. Unless Sebti's anxious look ... Elsewhere and present.
What did he want to tell us with his *Homme forgeron*?
Our elder was designing an unconvincing world system. Was he a visionary, or was he sinking into *madness* again?
Djaout and Skif and Touati and Laghouati and ... We guffawed at the bar, round after round, deaf to the call. Awkward, though. We recognised the insurgent poet. And got another round.
We were laughing in any case.
Hell, for him, is not just a literary device.
And when he says:

> 'The pathway of a struggle /
> Led me to madness /
> Plunged me into madness / ...'

we were convinced of the truth of this statement.
…
Knowing him better, I discovered an intellectual with a tortured soul, constantly questioning. Invited to a round table at our URASC research group on reformist movements in Islam, he gave a talk on 'the notion of alienation in Malek Bennabi'. Sadly I can't find the text now. His knowledge of Salafism amazed me, at a time when few of us cared about it.
'You've got to make a serious effort with Arabic,' he said to me during the coffee break. 'Otherwise you will always be incomplete.'

Nous nous sommes croisés de temps en temps…
Nous pensions le temps notre allié et le malmenions avec férocité.
…
Les occasions de rencontre devenaient de plus en plus rares.

L'homme qui s'est présenté à sa porte dans la nuit du 27 décembre 1993 n'était pas « affamé hagard et gémissant » avait pour armes autre chose qu'« un cri de douleur / et un bâton volé ». « Tôt ou tard », Sebti sait qu'il va venir commettre sa besogne.
Il l'attend.

… Quand je le relie aujourd'hui, je vois combien il habite ses vers au style sec, sarcastique parfois, toujours tendre. Les mots sont un patient arrachement à la solitude dans la réclusion (qui n'est pas celle du soufi, mais du récalcitrant) dans laquelle le poète se cantonne dans une tourmente permanente.

We crossed paths from time to time.
We thought of time as our ally and fiercely abused it.
…
Opportunities to meet were becoming increasingly scarce.

The man who appeared at his door on the night of 27 December 1993 was not 'hungry haggard and moaning' and had weapons other than 'a cry of pain / a stolen stick'. 'Sooner or later', Sebti knows he'll come to carry out his task.
He waits for him.

… When I reread it today, I see how much he fills his verse with a dry, sometimes sarcastic, always tender, style. Words are a patient wrench from the solitude of reclusion – not that of the Sufi but of the recalcitrant – which confines the poet in permanent tumult.

Lamento

Surgie de nulle part
et partout cette voix   ô

Peut-être râle dans les grottes du Dahra
au moment où tu traverses le quai de la gare

Artifice du refoulé surimposition d'image
tu ne crois plus aux revenants

Cadenassé dans ta chair tu avances
à mille pattes

Mise en scène au cordeau
les gosiers se posent sur le fil du rasoir

Intense l'éclat des visages déchirés par le texte

Atermoiement du discours

Lament

Out of nowhere
and everywhere this voice   O

Perhaps a groan in the Dahra caves
as you cross the station platform

Trick of the repressed, image superimposed
you no longer believe in ghosts

Chained in your flesh you crawl
hundred-legged beast

Careful staging
throats poised on the razor's edge

Intense shine of faces breached by the text

Speech postponed

Ordonnances

Soleil œil igné salon incendié
Rai devant seuil inondé

Avril refoule ton empressement
Regard sans sourciller

Novembre les amis disparus
Le comptoir se vide

Froid traîne son manteau neige sale
Gris de brume s'étire à l'horizon

Les préparatifs ne comblent pas l'absence

Ordinances

Sun fiery eye living room burned down
Ray before flooded doorstep

April rejects your eagerness
A look without blinking

Friends gone come November
The bar empties

Cold drags its dirty snow coat
Mist grey stretches out on the horizon

Preparations don't fill the absence

Proscription

Exil n'est plus coloquinte sous la dent
Anomalie sur formica
Dans l'arrière-salle d'un boui-boui emmitouflé

Personne ne s'attache comme autrefois

Ni pitié ni regret   mauvais sang
Chacun mène sa barque,   dit l'adage
Comme il peut

Comme le veut son étoile   / Y a-t-il étoile pour tous

Trouver des mots d'accueil   / pas escorte d'apparat
Des mots débarrassés d'effroi   / ni d'ordre ni demi
Des mots que la voix porte par tous les temps

Les quais encombrés des fantômes d'*Octobre*

Banishment

Exile is no longer biting   on bitter gourd
Anomaly on formica
In some shack's back room   muffled

No one's attached like before

Neither pity nor regret   bad blood
We each steer our boat,   goes the saying
As best we can

According to our stars   / Are there stars for everyone

Finding words of welcome   / not a majestic escort
Words stripped of terror   / neither watched nor implied
Words the voice carries come rain or shine

The docks are crowded with ghosts of *October*

Rengaine

Sombre cœur
Mer couleur de violette
Jamais brillante
      Dépassée
          L'ile lointaine

Les chants de l'exil déplorent un gâchis
Ce qui est ce qui est dit
Dégoût du pain et fiel
Rengaine réitérée

Amertume de l'étrange
        Obsession d'une patrie
Se perçoit à grand peine un lampadaire vacillant

Ici,
La nuit n'a pas de fin
Ni le froid
L'hiver dure plus que de saison

Mourir,
Pas question
Non.
Il n'en est pas question

C'est d'   Aimer
Mais le cœur où pâturent les gazelles ?

Refrain

Heavy heart
Violet-coloured sea
Never sparkling
                        Gone beyond
                                              Remote Island

Songs of exile deplore a waste
What is what is said
Disgust with bread and gall
Refrain repeated

Bitterness of the strange
                                Obsession with a homeland
A failing street lamp is just perceived

Here,
Night has no end
Nor the cold
Winter lasts longer than a season

To die,
No question
No.
There is no question of that

It's to   Love
But the heart where gazelles graze

Le feu

Soudain le feu   Hourra à la ronde   en plein
Midi   Exaltation où se glisse
Comme le reproche qui

Allait suivre
Au moment où cœur étincelle
Clame son désir d'étreindre

Mourir dans l'étonnement l'
Âme en alerte

Succession alors de vertiges
D'éclats au milieu des convives

Insensé à paraître dans le jour
D'évidences reniées sans succès

Effacement à l'approche de l'incendie
Au seuil altéré   ta mémoire

The fire

Suddenly the fire   Clamour all around   middle of
Midday   Excitement where it slips
Like the reproach which

Will follow
When the heart sparks
Claims its desire to embrace

To die in astonishment a
Soul on alert

A spate of dizziness then and
Flashes among the guests

Senseless to appear by day
Evidence denied in vain

Erasure as the fire nears
At the scarred threshold   your memory

Afterword

Habib Tengour, the poet, sociologist and anthropologist, is one of the most visionary voices of post-colonial Algeria. His poetry is steeped in the imaginative and cultural geography of the Maghrib, exile and dislocation only serving to heighten its musical registers. Often surrealist in nature, he has been dubbed a 'soufialist' by the literary critic Hédi Abdel Jaouad, yet running through his work is a core of nomadism. The figure of Ulysses has featured in most of his collections, a coat rack on which to hang his preoccupations with wanderlust and a search for home: a Ulysses seen through the keen sociological eyes of a poet brought up among Arab and Amazigh storytellers.

In this collection of poems, selected and translated by Will Harris and Delaina Haslam, voices drip between words, behind lines and through the pages. Habib Tengour speaks of the contradictions of his situation: a poet steeped in the poetics of anti-colonial resistance writing in the tongue of the coloniser. Born in French Algeria and brought up in France, he received his education in French from school through to university. Arabic on the other hand was the 'star nestled in [his] overcoat'; behind his French words lies the shadow of Arabic, of the voices from the marketplace, the voices of his people. Within his words he allows for this multiplicity of voices to be heard, and the poems chosen by Harris and Haslam replicate these voices, 'expressing [their] presence in a repaired tongue'.

The book opens with a piece that serves as the introduction to Tengour's collection *Consolatio*. It is about a writing desk – the base on which words are built and voices 'gleaned' – and takes the form of a series of interrogations on the nature of the craft of writing itself. The voice of the Algerian novelist, poet and playwright Mohammed Dib, is the first we encounter in a poem which plays around words and the loss of language. Settling on acrostics as the perfect medium ('automatic trigger') through which in a trance 'words … come and put themselves where they should be', the book progresses to an acrostic in admiration of Seamus Heaney. As Tengour never met Heaney, his voice is a voice from 'beyond' but still bearing with it the imprints of an unending 'furrow'. The long poem 'Le rempart de Sebti' is packed with voices: that of the pied noir poet Jean Sénac, as well as poet and chemist Youcef Sebti, both brutally murdered for refusing to censor their voices: Sénac for championing gay rights and Sebti's defiance in the face of totalitarianism.

> 'You've got to make a serious effort with Arabic,' he said to me during the coffee break. 'Otherwise you will always be incomplete.'

This is an injunction from Sebti which Tengour adhered to. Kateb Yacine's presence can also be felt in many of the poems, Tengour having paid tribute to the enormous influence Yacine's 1956 novel *Nedjma* has had on his own work and on the nascent revolutionary movement in 1950s Algeria. 'Out of nowhere / and everywhere': Tengour amplifies, delves into and broadcasts voices whose registers are so familiar to him they help his exile 'find a route back in song'.

If Habib Tengour carries with him the shadow of other voices and languages, so do the two translators and it is interesting to read these translations with an ear open to the linguistic registers of Indonesia and Spain lurking behind Harris and Haslam's choice of words. In their introduction, the two translators write of how they worked on each poem together: a collaboration which while denying the reader the opportunity to pin a specific translation to a specific translator, is all the stronger for the blending of voices. These translations are richer for having travelled through two minds. There is nothing more rewarding than peeling back the words of a poem in a different language, of entering the scaffolding of the lines and of grappling with the essence of a work as it moves towards finding utterance in a new language. As Tengour says, writing itself is an act of translation. The process of searching for words in any language is the process of translation itself, as all languages are grappling with making aspects of life and memory tangible. Harris and Haslam's translations are rich and varied, capturing the multiple shadows behind Tengour's French and rendering them into an English that envelopes and cradles their complexity.

In a 2021 interview at Iowa, when asked what excited him most about the future, Tengour's answer was immediate: it was the youth, the next generation, their enthusiasm and engagement which filled him with hope. Tengour has had a long and very fruitful collaboration with his translator Pierre Joris; the pair met in 1977 and have worked closely since. But it seems right that a new and younger generation of translators are now turning their focus on Tengour's work. These poems selected by Harris and Haslam from *Consolatio* have not been previously translated into English. It is fitting that the first book of translations of Tengour's poetry to be published in this country should emerge from the skillful pens of this new and exciting partnership.

Shash Trevett

Algerian poet and anthropologist Habib Tengour was born in 1947 in Mostaganem. He has more than 15 works of poetry, prose, theatre, and essays to his name, published by Algerian and French publishing houses and in poetry magazines (including *Poetic Action*, *PO&sie*, *La translattière* and *Bacchanales*).

His work has been translated into English, German, Arabic, Italian, Macedonian, and Dutch. He divides his time between Algeria and France, and between his anthropological research and his literary work. He translates poets from English (Pierre Joris, Charles Bernstein, Cole Swensen), German (Hans Thill), and Arabic (Saadi Youssef, Chawki Abdelamir, Moncef Louhaïbi).

He won the Dante European Poetry Prize in 2016 for his entire poetic work.

He edits the 'Poèmes du Monde' series published by APIC (Algiers); the first edition of seven collections of poetry launched in 2018.

Will Harris is a London-based writer and editor. His debut poetry book *RENDANG* (2020) was a Poetry Book Society Choice, was shortlisted for the T.S. Eliot Prize, and won the Forward Prize for Best First Collection. His second book of poems, *Brother Poem*, will be published by Granta Books in 2023.

Delaina Haslam studied English and French and has lived in France and Spain. After working in editing roles she retrained in translation and specialises in the field of sociology. She has been involved in several collaborations including a series of Poetry Translation Centre workshops on francophone African poets.

Shash Trevett is a Tamil from Sri Lanka who came to the UK to escape the civil war. She is a poet and a translator of Tamil poetry into English. Her pamphlet *From a Borrowed Land* was published by Smith|Doorstop. Shash was a 2021 Visible Communities Translator in Residence at the National Centre for Writing and is a Ledbury Critic. She is a Board Member of Modern Poetry in Translation.

About the Poetry Translation Centre

Set up in 2004, the Poetry Translation Centre is the only UK organisation dedicated to translating, publishing and promoting contemporary poetry from Africa, Asia, the Middle East and Latin America. We introduce extraordinary poets from around the world to new audiences through books, online resources and bilingual events. We champion diversity and representation in the arts and forge enduring relations with diaspora communities in the UK. We explore the craft of translation through our long-running programme of workshops which are open to all.

The Poetry Translation Centre is based in London and is an Arts Council National Portfolio organisation. To find out more about us, including how you can support our work, please visit:

www.poetrytranslation.org.

About the World Poet Series

The *World Poet Series* offers an introduction to some of the world's most exciting contemporary poets in an elegant pocket-sized format. The books are presented as bilingual editions, with the English and original-language text displayed side by side. They include specially commissioned translations and completing each book is an afterword essay by a UK-based poet, responding to the translations.